WORLD ECONOMY EXPLAINED

Banks and Banking

Sean Connolly

FRANKLIN WATTS
LONDON•SYDNEY

An Appleseed Editions book

First published in 2010 by Franklin Watts
338 Euston Road, London NW1 3BH

Franklin Watts Australia
Hachette Children's Books
Level 17/207 Kent St, Sydney, NSW 2000

© 2010 Appleseed Editions

Created by Appleseed Editions Ltd,
Well House, Friars Hill, Guestling,
East Sussex TN35 4ET

Designed by Helen James
Edited by Mary-Jane Wilkins
Picture research by Su Alexander

ISBN 978 1 4451 0040 1

Dewey Classification: 332.1

A CIP catalogue for this book is available from the British Library.

Photograph acknowledgements
page 7 Sebastiao Moreira/epa/Corbis; 9 Ted Spiegel/Corbis; 10 Historical Picture
Archive/Corbis; 12 The London Art Archive/Alamy; 14 Paul Hutley;Eye Ubiquitous/
Corbis; 16 FLAB/Alamy; 18 Justin Lane/epa/Corbis; 21 Phil Noble/Reuters/Corbis;
23 Getty Images; 25 Richard Pohle/Rex Features; 26 Mary Evans Picture Library/
Alamy; 29 Phillimon Bulaway/epa/Corbis; 31 Jim West/Alamy; 32 Jason Reed/
Reuters/Corbis; 35 Richard Levine/Alamy; 36 Andy Rain/epa/Corbis; 39 Michel
Setboun/Corbis; 41 Mike Theiler/epa/Corbis; 43 Joseph Van Os/Getty Images
Front cover Justin Lane/epa/Corbis

Printed in China

Franklin Watts is a division of Hachette Children's Books,
an Hachette UK company.
www.hachette.co.uk

Contents

What has happened to the banks?

For years people believed the world of banking to be cautious, respectable and unchanging. All that changed in 2008, when worldwide banking crises hit the headlines. Banks were accused of behaving recklessly in previous years, lending money to borrowers who had little chance of paying it back.

As house prices dropped (along with some borrowers' chances of ever repaying their loans) the banks started to lose money. And with these losses came another blow: many savers began to fear that their money was no longer safe in banks, so they decided to withdraw their deposits.

Suddenly the banks' image changed. People began to see that they depended on a steady balance of lending and borrowing to make a profit, or even to operate at all. If that balance is lost – either because borrowers cannot repay their debts or because savers take out their money – then the banks' business falls apart.

The credit crunch

This unsettling train of events continued for weeks and months, as bank after bank around the world admitted that they were having difficulties. Then came the unthinkable news – some of the biggest names in banking were going out of business. And if banks went under, who knew what would happen to the people and businesses that depended on those banks...

Before long, people saw that the problems facing banks spilled over into everyone's life, in one way or another. Governments were forced to spend vast sums to protect their citizens from the effects of the credit crunch, as the crisis came to be called (see pages 30-33). Some governments even took over banks that would otherwise have failed. In a few short months, banking outsiders learned a great deal about how banks and the banking industry operated.

New explanations

How could an industry change its character so dramatically in such a short time? Or did it? Perhaps people had misunderstood the nature of banking and the risks associated with it, and the credit crunch simply exposed the truth. On the other hand, it could be that the banking system will remain stable, and that the credit crisis will prove to be a temporary – but dramatic – exception to this trend. This book will help you draw your own conclusions.

Brazilian financial traders react to bad economic news from the United States in January 2008 in scenes that reflect the drama of the world banking crisis.

The background to banking

The word 'bank' goes back hundreds of years, but the idea of banking is much older, dating back nearly 4000 years. Some historians believe that temples in ancient times also served as a type of bank. Even before people had money, they needed somewhere safe to keep their valuable goods.

Temples were ideal for this purpose because they were built well and were protected from robbers and invaders. Local farmers could store grain, jewels and other cherished items in a temple, probably in exchange for an offering.

More detailed evidence of this comes from ancient Babylon, which was one of the first civilizations to have written records. Hammurabi's Code, a type of constitution that is one of the world's first legal documents (dating from about 1760 BC), includes laws about banking operations. These laws refer to loans that Babylonian priests made to local merchants.

Trade routes

The ancient Greeks developed banking further. Like other civilizations, the Greeks spread their influence through military force. But they also used trade as a way of making contact with other peoples, and their influence spread because of their skilful trading practices. Like the Babylonians, they first used temples as banking centres where they could exchange currencies, take deposits and make loans.

The Greeks also developed the idea of credit. A merchant travelling to one Greek port could sell his goods and receive a note of credit from the buyer. The merchant could then exchange or cash in this note at another port. The system was convenient and reduced the risks of travelling with large amounts of gold or coins.

The Romans, whose governing skills maintained their enormous empire, imposed rules and regulations on banking transactions. They also introduced interest (see page 13) as an important aspect of business dealings. But as the Roman Empire came under threat from the fourth century AD, people began using cash again because it seemed safer.

Crusades and coffee

After the fall of the Roman Empire in the late fifth century, Europe largely abandoned banking in favour of more traditional, barter-style dealings. Banking only reappeared about seven centuries later as a way of raising money for the Crusades. The trading city-states of Italy, such as Venice and Florence, became the leading centres of European banking. Deals were struck with the lender and the borrower sitting on opposite sides of a cloth-covered board (called a banco). Some banking families, such as the Medici of Florence, became enormously wealthy and powerful.

Medallions depict leading members of the Medici, the famous Florentine banking family whose gold florins (the smaller coins) were common coins throughout Europe during the fifteenth and sixteenth centuries.

Modern banking aimed at helping businesses and individuals began in northern Europe. The coffee houses of London and Amsterdam became meeting places for informal banking meetings during the sixteenth and seventeenth centuries. The Royal Exchange, established in London in 1565, and the Amsterdam Exchange Bank (founded in 1609) made England and the Netherlands important banking centres.

Europe remained the leading banking region for several centuries, strengthened by exploration and increasing trade in new European colonies. But it was the Industrial Revolution that brought about the real banking explosion during the eighteenth and nineteenth centuries. In northern Europe, then in North America and beyond, banks funded the massive increase in trade brought about by new

The architect John Soane redeveloped the Bank of England buildings in the early nineteenth century. Banknotes were issued in the Great Hall (above), where traders spent their working days making deals.

factories and manufacturing techniques. When we look back at some of the banking images from that era, banking seems backward and primitive – with clerks using quill pens to write long documents by candlelight. But many of the banking practices that are now carried out online or over the phone were in place by the mid-nineteenth century. Business owners could raise funds for new investments, savers could choose from different accounts and people could turn to banks to help them take the first step towards owning a home.

With all these developments came the banking troubles that have caused headlines in the twenty-first century – poor risks, overstretched banks and borrowers defaulting on their mortgage repayments.

YOUR MONEY'S WORTH

Then and now

What do you suppose drove people to set up the predecessors of our banks thousands of years ago? Are any of those reasons still relevant today?

Saved by the geese

Although the Greeks and Romans helped to develop banking practices and had wide experience of using interest in their dealings, many of their transactions were still made in cash. And that cash – in the form of gold and silver coins – had to be stored somewhere safe. The Romans kept their reserves on the Capitol, one of the seven hills of Rome.

This storehouse of money was a target for the many invaders who attempted to capture the city. In 390 BC, warriors from Gaul (now France) attacked the city and made their way to the Capitol. Luckily for the Romans, the invaders disturbed the geese that lived there, and the cackling alerted the Roman defenders, who drove off the Gauls. The grateful Romans built a shrine to Moneta, their goddess of warning.

This action had another legacy, giving us the words 'money' and 'mint' – both of which are named after Moneta.

How banks work

In William Shakespeare's most famous play, *Hamlet*, the character Polonius offers this advice to his son Laertes: 'neither a borrower nor a lender be.' And yet, that is exactly how banks operate – they borrow money from some customers and lend money to others. They pay to borrow the first set of money but charge more to lend the second set. The difference is profit.

This early sixteenth-century painting, The Money Lender and His Wife, *depicts the conflict Europeans felt between banking wealth and anti-lending attitudes. The lender counts jewels while his wife reads a religious book.*

Making a profit

Every business needs to earn a profit – or make money – if it is to continue operating. It is easy to understand how many businesses do this because we can touch, look at or taste what they sell. It is also easy to grasp how these products or services are produced – and at what cost.

Imagine a small company that sells home-baked cakes in a country town. The husband and wife who run the company first need to buy the ingredients – flour, milk, eggs, sugar, butter and so on – to make the cakes. They then need to work out the cost of heating their oven long enough to bake all the cakes. Then they calculate the transport costs (petrol and so on) for taking the cakes to the different shops that will sell them. Finally, they consider how much they will pay the shopkeepers to sell those cakes.

Once the small cake-making company has worked out all these costs, they then decide on a price for each cake. If that price is £1 more than the other total costs, then the profit the company makes is £1 per cake. Using similar calculations, car-makers, film studios, restaurants and hotels can fix on a price that covers their own costs and adds a little extra as profit.

Paying and charging interest

Banks work in the same way, although their product is money itself. The extra money they pay to savers in return for using their money is called interest. The same term, interest, also describes the money they charge people who borrow from them. See how the system works in the example below.

A teenager opens a bank account so she can save the £1000 she was given for her eighteenth birthday. The bank offers her three per cent annual interest on her deposit (the £1000) so after a year (provided she leaves the money in the bank) her £1000 will be worth £1030.

The £30 interest is the fee that the bank paid her for using her money during the year. At the same time, another teenager approaches the bank hoping to borrow £1000 to buy a used car. The bank agrees to lend her the money, but it will charge her seven per cent annual interest as a fee for the loan. After a year this teenager will have paid the bank £1070 – in this case, the £70 is the fee that the customer paid the bank.

Tower 42 is one of London's highest skyscrapers. It was originally called the NatWest Tower because it was built by the National Westminster Bank.

If we imagine further that the bank used the same £1000 that it received from the first woman to lend to the second woman, then the result is easy to follow. The bank has made a £40 profit: the £70 fee it received minus the £30 that it paid out.

Economy of scale

Looking at the example above, the amount of money involved might seem too small to keep a bank working. That is true. But even the smallest banks deal with much more money than a thousand pounds here and there. If just 100 people deposit £10,000 each – maybe not all at once, but over a period of time – then a bank ends up with a million pounds. And if the borrowing and lending rates (the interest percentages) are the same as in the example, then the bank makes £40,000 profit from the money.

YOUR MONEY'S WORTH

Different rules?

Polonius's advice to his son raises an interesting question: if a person shouldn't either borrow or lend money, then why should a company such as a bank do this?

Do you think that the rules of behaviour for individuals should be different from the rules for companies?

The example can be taken further. Think about how many people live in the UK, and how many of them earn money and set some of it aside – to pay for university fees, to save for holidays or simply for a rainy day. There are millions of savers who do this. Then imagine the difference between the money the banks pay out (to savers) and the money they collect back (from borrowers). These amounts run to millions of pounds.

Even if the banks are making millions of pounds of profit, rather than just £40 here and there, the basic system of making a profit remains. Shakespeare's character Polonius quoted on page 12 might have been cautious, but banks usually manage to remain cautious while still making a profit. Unless, of course, a widespread crisis leads people to worry about just how safe their money is...

Just your type?

Although the banking industry may be thousands of years old, it would be unrecognizable in its present form to those first priests and temple guardians who stored farmers' grain and jewels. Those first bankers had no concept of money, let alone mortgages, cash machines, online payments or any of the features of modern banking.

Yet modern banks still need to offer customers some of the advantages the temple keepers and other early bankers provided. For one thing, people still want security – a safe place in which to deposit their valuables. They also value fairness and predictability. And when

Unlike the stately, sombre banks of the early nineteenth century, modern bank branches are bright and welcoming. They even advertise some of their products in their windows.

the modern banking world faces a major crisis, people's fears and complaints centre on these age-old concerns. It is only when people's confidence returns that banks can expect to operate smoothly and profitably again.

The banks must retain their core qualities of security, fairness and reliability. If we bear this in mind, it is easier to understand the banking industry overall. Banks sometimes seem to be evolving so fast that we can't keep track of new developments, leaving people with unanswered questions such as 'What's wrong with chequebooks?' or 'Will people use cash in the future?' But we can understand the industry by remembering its basic aims, no matter how those aims are achieved.

Two main types of bank

The BBC, which reports many times every day on banking and other economic subjects, aims to present news clearly, using terms that most people understand. Banks became news subjects more regularly than usual when what has become known as the credit crunch took hold in 2008. As a result, the BBC compiled a glossary of credit crunch terms on its website. Internet users can quickly check the meaning of the financial language that economic reporters sometimes use.

The BBC glossary reminds readers of something basic: there are two main types of bank, and others are simply versions of the two. The two basic types are commercial banks and investment banks, and the boundaries between these categories can sometimes be blurred.

Commercial banks are the banks that most people recognize – the type that has branches on most high streets. They serve the needs of most individuals, families and small businesses. People set up current accounts and savings accounts in commercial banks. They also go to these banks for loans to buy cars, to have building work done on their houses or to take out a mortgage loan to buy a house.

The clue to what investment banks do lies in the word 'invest'. These banks help large businesses raise money in stocks and other investments. They deal with businesses and not individuals: for example, an investment bank might offer advice to companies on how to join forces with other companies, or on how one company could buy out another.

Other types of bank

The banking industry has been changing in ways that have blurred the lines between commercial and investment banks. Some of the largest banks, for example, have both commercial and investment branches. The American bank Citigroup has different arms which deal with each type of banking business. Other types of bank, which go by different

Appearances can be deceptive: this is the towering former HQ of Bear Stearns Bank in New York City. Once one of the world's leading investment banks, it went out of business dramatically in 2008.

Web accounts

Like many other industries, banks have begun to use the Internet as a way of expanding their business. Customers can go online to find bank details that would otherwise involve making a visit to the branch, phoning them or writing a letter. Many banking transactions, such as transfers and withdrawals, can now be done online, at any time of the day or night. Some new banks exist only on the Internet.

Egg and First Direct are Internet banks that have no high street branches at all. In fact, they have no real branches or buildings. They claim to be able to offer customers better rates because their overheads are so low. Other banks have a larger number of staff and hundreds of branches to maintain. The online banks offer 24-hour convenience instead of bricks and mortar.

names, turn out to be very similar to either commercial or investment banks. Private banks, for example, deal with the assets of very rich people. So at first they seem to be a type of commercial bank. But the vast fortunes of some wealthy people are similar to the amounts of money that large companies have to spend – putting these funds to their best use is similar to offering investment advice to big businesses.

Offshore banks are based outside the legal boundaries of countries that have strict banking regulations so, in this sense, offshore means simply abroad or in another country. Many of these banks are based in Switzerland, the Cayman Islands in the Caribbean, or the Channel Islands – all of which are known for having low taxes and few banking rules and regulations.

With many people now blaming banks for leading the world into the credit crunch (see pages 30-33), each type of bank is stressing how secure – rather than profitable – their products are.

Safe as houses

For most people, the largest

investment they will ever make is in their house. Owning a house is a deep-rooted desire for many people, particularly in the English-speaking world: the saying 'an Englishman's home is his castle' sums this up.

In addition to giving people a feeling of power and security, owning a home offers them an opportunity to make money. Decades can pass during which house prices rise. Just staying in the same house can give people the chance to see their initial investment (the price they paid for the house) increase. Then, if people sell because their children have moved away and they want to move somewhere smaller, or if they move from an expensive city to a more rural location, they can reap the benefits of this increase in value when they sell the house.

House ownership has all sorts of effects on the wider, national economy. In good times, when many people move into new houses or buy older ones to renovate them, thousands of people find work in what is called the housing industry. House designers, builders, plumbers, electricians and estate agents all benefit from a housing boom: similarly, they suffer when there is a slump in the housing market because of falling prices.

Boom and bust

By late 2008, international experts agreed that the world economy was in crisis. And most also agreed that the trigger that started the crisis was the American housing economy. For many years, US house prices had increased: for example, a buyer who took out a $100,000 (£65,000) mortgage on a $130,000 (£84,500) house knew that the value of that house would go up. So if he had to sell the house – in

order to work somewhere else or because he had lost his job – he would get back more than the £84,500. That also meant that he could easily pay back what he owed on the mortgage and still end up with some extra money.

However, if house prices begin to fall, people may find that the amount of money they have borrowed to buy their house (their mortgage) ends up being greater than the money they would get from selling the house. This is called negative equity.

By 2006 American house prices had begun to dip and then to fall quickly in many areas. It turned out that when things had been good, many banks had lent money to people who were thought to be bad risks (for example, because they might lose their jobs or because their health was poor). These loans are known as sub-prime mortgages. By 2006 and 2007, many of the borrowers were unable to meet their

'For sale' and 'To let' signs outside flats in Manchester in northern England in January 2008 – indications of how bad the housing market had become. Just three years earlier, the same flats would have been sold or let within days.

Housing helpers

Poorer British people found it difficult to open bank accounts in the eighteenth century. As banks are the places people traditionally go to take out loans to buy or build houses, poor people had little opportunity of owning their own homes. Many rented their homes instead.

Some people found a way round the problem by setting up organizations of their own which helped to provide funds for housing. These organizations were owned by their members and called building societies. They offered a popular way for less well off people to borrow money – and to invest their savings. By the mid-nineteenth century, there were more than 2500 building societies in Britain. Similar organizations developed in other countries. Sometimes they were called building societies (as in Australia) and sometimes they had other names, for example savings and loan associations in America.

British building societies faced more restrictions than banks, so they often struggled to compete with them. Some closed down; some merged to become stronger and others changed their rules to become banks. To do that, they had to ask the permission of their members (who were actually the owners). By 2008, there were fewer than 60 building societies in Great Britain.

mortgage payments and banks began losing millions of dollars. The sub-prime crisis spread through the US banking industry and then through nearly every other area linked to money and finance. By the middle of 2008, economic stories dominated news headlines and people's conversation around the world. Suddenly it seemed as though the world economy was simply a house of cards.

Americans elected a new president later in 2008. They chose Barack Obama because he promised change – especially change from the way that the previous president, George W. Bush, had seemed to do nothing to improve the housing market.

Opposite: many unemployed people in the US had to live in basic shacks, like these in Seattle, Washington, during the worst years of the Depression.

Personal account

FALLING VALUES

Ninety-year-old Jim still has clear memories of his youth near the American city of Boston. He lived through the Great Depression and points out that negative equity is not something new.

'My dad died in the influenza epidemic of 1918 so my mother had to bring up seven children herself. I was the youngest but by the time I was four or five, my eldest two brothers were out working to support the family. They saved enough for a down payment on a house – before that we had rented. The mortgage took effect exactly a week before Black Friday – the day that really started the Depression in October 1929.

'More of the family grew old enough to work – including me – but jobs were hard to find. Those monthly mortgage payments were tough, especially because the value of the house had plummeted along with everything else at the start of the Depression. We would still owe thousands of dollars, a lot of money then, if we had tried to sell the house. So we kept on paying. Each year we had a letter from the town manager telling us how much the house was worth. It only regained its October 1929 value in 1947, eighteen years after we bought it. We made the last mortgage payment two years later.'

At the centre of things

Entire countries rely on banks, just as individuals and companies do. Most countries have a central bank, which influences how that country's economy works. The first such central bank – and still one of the most famous – is the Bank of England, which was founded in 1694. The central bank of the United States is called the Federal Reserve, or the Fed.

Guiding the economy

The Bank of England, the Fed and other central banks perform a number of jobs. One of the most important is fighting inflation, which is the trend for money (including people's earnings) to lose value. Reducing the amount of money circulating in a country can lower inflation. Central banks can control inflation by selling government bonds: this causes interest rates to rise because more of these bonds become available. The extra bonds need to have something special – usually higher interest rates – to make people want to buy them. Banks then need to raise their interest rates to compete with the bonds.

When interest rates rise (making loans more expensive), there is less borrowing, which in turn leads to less money in the economy – and lower inflation. Central banks can also reduce the money supply by doing an obvious thing: printing less money.

Central banks can also do the opposite – buy back bonds to lower interest rates – if things go too far. Lower interest rates mean more borrowing, which can often lead to companies expanding and providing more jobs for people. The central banks need to use great skill to maintain the right balance, so that prices remain stable (controlling inflation) while as many people as possible have jobs.

Eddie George (left) was Governor of the Bank of England from 1993 to 2003. He is shown here with Gordon Brown, then Chancellor of the Exchequer.

The last resort

Central banks have another important task: to back up the entire banking system. They are often called 'lenders of last resort', because commercial banks can turn to central banks to help them operate smoothly. Money is always entering and leaving commercial banks and this flow is dictated by customers. For example, if people are withdrawing money from their bank accounts, more money flows out from a bank: money flows in when more people are saving (investing).

If there is an imbalance (not enough money in the bank), then a commercial bank can borrow from a central bank. This borrowing is common and helps to sustain people's confidence in banks generally. As with any bank borrowing, interest must be paid. The interest charged to banks by the Bank of England, for example, is called the base rate. The amount of interest that commercial banks charge (or pay) customers rises or falls in line with this base rate. All these responsibilities mean that central banks play an important role in trying to resolve major financial crises – both nationally and internationally.

YOUR MONEY'S WORTH

An independent Bank of England?

Soon after the Labour party won the 1997 general election, Gordon Brown (then Chancellor of the Exchequer) made the Bank of England independent. Before that, the bank had followed government policy in raising or lowering interest rates.

Do you think the Bank of England should be independent and not swayed one way or another by politicians? Or should it follow the instructions of the people elected to guide the country?

When things go wrong

There were some disastrous economic periods in the early twentieth century which show how economies can become uncontrollable. The lessons learned in the wake of these periods have helped central banks to assume some of their modern roles. The banking industry was partly to blame for these crises, but, more importantly, it emerged with the tools to help prevent such severe problems in the future.

In Germany prices had risen so much by 1923 that people bought and sold money by weight. The sign shows that paper money was worth more than old bones, but less than rags.

Personal account

WHEN MONEY LOSES VALUE

Economist Gerhard Bry quoted Doctor Frieda Wunderlick in his book Wages in Germany 1871-1945 *(Princeton University Press, 1960). Here Doctor Wunderlick gives an account of how Germany's hyperinflation in the 1920s affected her personally.*

'As soon as I received my salary I rushed out to buy the daily necessities. My salary... was just enough to buy one loaf of bread and a small piece of cheese or oatmeal. On one occasion I had to refuse to give a lecture at a Berlin city college because I could not be assured that the fee would cover the subway fare to the classroom, and it was too far to walk. On another occasion, a private lesson I gave to the wife of a farmer was somewhat better paid – by one loaf of bread for the hour.'

Runaway inflation

One of the most dramatic examples of how things can go wrong arose in Germany just after the First World War. The main victors in the war, Great Britain and France, insisted that Germany pay reparations to them so that they could rebuild their economies. For two and a half years, they worked out how much they would charge Germany. They reached a figure of £6.6 billion (at least £210 billion in today's money).

It was difficult for Germany to repay this money because it, too, had been hit hard by the war. Nevertheless, Germany came close to paying the first instalment of £2 billion later that year. After that, though, it became almost impossible to continue repaying the debt. When France claimed some of Germany's most important industrial land in compensation, the situation became really bad in Germany.

The German government faced a choice: it could either raise taxes enormously (an unpopular move which would lead to defeat at the next election) or simply print more money. It chose to print money, which at first seemed to help. But then ordinary people realized that there was little or no backing for the extra money: governments traditionally held stores of gold to match (or back) the paper money that they printed.

Ordinary Germans soon realized that something was wrong and that the value of their currency, the mark, was falling. As they were forbidden to withdraw money in the form of gold, the mark fell further: the fall was accelerated by panic as much as Germany's poor economic position.

Massive inflation took hold, so that the value of the mark fell first by the day, then by the hour and then by the minute. Some economists use the 'loaf of bread' index to describe a currency's value: ie how much a loaf of bread costs in a particular country. In 1918, just as the war ended, a loaf cost 0.6 marks: by July 1922 it cost nearly 3500 marks and by November 1923 it was 200 billion marks.

The Great Depression

The Great Depression lasted from 1929 until the start of the Second World War, and was a time of great economic hardship. Banks were also the victims: many of them went out of business as people lost confidence and tried to withdraw all their savings.

On top of that, many people found it difficult to repay loans they had taken out from banks. And then, because ordinary people were so affected by the downturn and job losses, companies sold (and produced) fewer goods.

The Depression began in the United States but spread to most parts of the world, especially to countries that relied on manufacturing goods. Today's economists, bankers and political leaders all know that the world would suffer greatly if the Depression of the 1930s was repeated.

Finding solutions

Germany's period of hyperinflation and the Great Depression of the following decade were devastating, but they helped the world's organizations find safeguards against a repeat of such turmoil. The recent history of the African country of Zimbabwe shows how hyperinflation can ruin a thriving economy. And the credit crunch of the twenty-first century – like every recession that has preceded it – is constantly examined to see whether it could tip into a depression.

Modern central bank responsibilities and banking regulations (see pages 24-25) have done much to protect the world from such excesses. But the banking industry still keeps a watchful eye on economic developments…

Today there is a modern equivalent of 1920s Germany in the African country of Zimbabwe. Here people face rocketing prices. This shopper holds a loaf of bread in one hand, and the amount of money needed to pay for it in the other.

The credit crunch

The international economic crisis which began in 2008 looks likely to be the most severe crisis since the depression of the 1930s. Several times since the Great Depression, countries (and in some cases, the world economy) have faced recessions.

Economists have a definition of these mini-depressions: a recession is a period of reduced economic activity lasting for at least six months. No one now doubts that the crisis which began in 2008 is a full-scale recession. All the different elements that are known as 'economic activity' have been affected in most countries: national economic growth, personal income, sales of goods and services, and the quantity of goods being manufactured. The end result for many people is less work and maybe no job at all.

From risk to failure

Part of the problem surrounding the credit crunch is the complicated nature of the modern banking industry. By the twenty-first century, the traditional system of using investors' savings (deposits) to match loans (credit) was only part of the picture. Banks also used their money to invest in other projects: sometimes they invested in complicated housing-loan programmes set up by other banks.

These bank-to-bank investments were fine while the housing market was thriving. Borrowers were able to pay back mortgages, the banks that lent money to those borrowers made a profit on their repayments and other banks (which had investments tied to those deals) also made a profit. When things went wrong in 2006 and 2007, the knock-on effect was sudden and dramatic. Some of the high-risk borrowers failed to meet their mortgage repayments. They lost their homes when the banks foreclosed. But these banks could not release the money tied up in the houses because the price of houses was falling. As a result, they began to struggle and fail, which in turn led to other banks (which had invested in those complicated house-loan deals) facing trouble. Their money was tied up in what became known as toxic debts, which might never become money again. And when savers at these banks wanted to withdraw their deposits, the banks were often unable to find the money.

Without sufficient money, banks became unable or unwilling to take a chance by lending. This extended not just to individuals and companies needing to borrow money, but to other banks. Usually banks are prepared to lend to each other in an international market. There is even a special interest rate for these arrangements, called the London Interbank Offered Rate (Libor). As the credit crunch grew worse, this rate became higher and higher. Banks began to

Foreclosure sale signs have become more common as the housing slump continues. Banks foreclose on a mortgage or other house loan and take over the property if the borrower can no longer make repayments.

The imposing Washington HQ of Fannie Mae gives no sign of how close the American superbank came to collapsing in 2008.

fail, squeezed by the problems they faced from their borrowers and their own difficulties in raising money. The term 'bank failure' was a scary reminder of the Great Depression: people began to fear the worst. Something had to be done to restore order and confidence.

New rescue plans

The United States, the UK and other governments spent the last months of 2008 devising rescue plans and financial bail-outs (see pages 40-41). These might slow the decline and possibly reverse it. But how many experts predicted the severity and length of the crisis?

YOUR MONEY'S WORTH

Blowing the whistle

Many experts blame risky housing investments by banks for the toxic debts that triggered the credit crunch – and recession. Should banks be banned from making such investments in the future,

or can they be trusted to behave more sensibly? And would other problems arise if there was such a ban?

The bigger they are, the harder they fall

One of the most shocking aspects of the credit crunch has been the way in which leading banks and other financial institutions have crashed. The banking industry relies on an element of public trust. So when some of the biggest names in banking are hit, the industry – and the whole world – suffers.

The UK hit the headlines with one such crisis in September 2007, when Northern Rock collapsed (see pages 40-41). By that point it was clear that the financial crisis was international: bad news in the United States travelled to other countries and the international effects of the news bounced back to America. The result was a staggering loss of confidence in the world's financial industry.

The trigger for the sudden run of bad news – trouble with US housing loans – continued to affect the wider world economy. By the middle of 2008, two huge organizations sponsored by the US government – nicknamed Fannie Mae and Freddie Mac – were close to collapse. The pair had acted as superbanks for decades, buying mortgages from lending banks and selling them on to investors. This gave banks confidence to continue lending, but the housing crisis hit Fannie Mae and Freddie Mac hard. On 7 September, the US government stepped in and took control of the pair: the move is expected to cost US taxpayers billions of dollars.

Just a week later Lehman Brothers, one of the oldest banks in the United States, went out of business. It was unable to cope with $60 billion (£40 billion) of bad debts that it was unlikely to retrieve. This was just one of the important banks to collapse during the credit crisis. Others have failed in nearly every major country and experts fear more failures will come.

Will people ever trust the experts, with their promises of possible recovery, again? The banking industry hopes so. In some ways, the modern credit crunch resembles the Great Depression, but in others the world has moved on and there are new problems which need new solutions.

The human dimension

Ordinary people have always benefited or suffered along with the wider economy. Investments soar – and everyone becomes better off – during a boom, while belt-tightening during a recession is just as noticeable. But a major downturn such as the credit crunch which began in August 2008 affects people on a daily basis, heightening fears and leading to big personal losses.

Two-way street

Unfortunately, many people learn about the relationship between the wider economy and their own lives the hard way. It might be easy to grasp how banks (and even central banks) need to match their income with spending – just as anyone managing a household must. It is often harder for people to understand why they suffer when the banks start facing problems themselves.

The truth is that the wider economy reflects the financial circumstances of the millions of people living in a country, and at the same time it affects those same millions. Banks are part of the process, just as other financial institutions (such as stock markets) and governments are.

The relationship between individuals and wider organizations is a two-way street. For example, many banks in the United States, the UK and other countries lent money to people who were considered high risk. Many of these borrowers found it impossible to meet their loan repayments when house prices began to fall during 2006.

So banks were stuck with these unpaid mortgages, which are sometimes called toxic debts because they are so harmful to the banks. To protect themselves in future the banks began to make it much harder to borrow

money – that way they would not have to face more toxic debts
in future. During the process, many reliable individuals and
companies found it impossible to take out loans.

Frozen assets

Sometimes we can trace difficulties directly from international level
down to national and then local level, and finally to their effects on
individuals. Iceland is a good example. In the 1990s, Iceland became
prosperous based on a government policy that allowed companies
(and banks) a great deal of freedom, which meant few safeguards
for investors' funds. Icelandic banks were able to attract vast
amounts of money from foreign investors. Many of these investors
were British councils and charities, eager to make their money
go further by taking advantage of the high interest rates that
the Icelandic banks were offering.

*Cutbacks caused by the credit
crunch forced the New York Public
Library to sell its Donnell Library
branch to a hotel developer in
2008. Similar stories are common
around the world as the credit
crunch continues.*

Personal account

NOT JUST THE BIG BOSSES

Ian has worked in banking for nearly 30 years, starting straight after university. 'It's funny – I had never imagined myself as a banker, but Lloyds hired me because of my language degree (in German).'

Ian found that he thrived in the world of banking – not because he was a high-flying risk-taker, but because he could see how banks could help imaginative people set up funds to start new businesses. Ian has worked with several banks during his career, using his language skills to work in several foreign cities. All the time, though, he was keen to return to Britain, making it a base for his young family. He aimed to cash in some banking shares he had earned as part of his salary in the 1990s. Overnight those shares became virtually worthless: Ian had earned them while working for Lehman Brothers, the American bank that collapsed dramatically in September 2008. He also recalls that in the high-risk days of the 1990s, he had warned the bank about some of its loans, but that people had ignored him.

In early 2008, Wiltshire County Council invested £12 million in Heritable Bank, which is owned by the Icelandic Landsbanki Island Group. The £12 million was part of its operating fund, made up of money received from council tax as well as money from central government. Landsbanki is one of several Icelandic banks that failed in October 2008. The effects of this failure extended beyond Iceland. By late October, Wiltshire County Council was reporting that it could only expect to receive one third (£4 million) of its Heritable investment back. It was obvious that cuts would need to be made – and fast.

One area already under threat was day-care for mentally handicapped people in the county. Several day centres faced closure because of a lack of funding, and many outings – to swimming pools, riding centres and other recreation centres – had already been stopped. The mentally handicapped, as well as their carers and the staff working in day centres, faced a period of uncertainty because of the Icelandic banking crisis. Schools, libraries and old-people's homes across the county – and in many other counties – faced similar cuts and an uncertain future.

Events like these have been repeated around the world when things go wrong. They demonstrate that whether we like it or not, we are all part of a global economy.

Opposite: the end of an era – the last of Britain's 807 branches of Woolworths stores closed in January 2009. The chain of shops was one of the most famous victims of the credit crunch.

YOUR MONEY'S WORTH

Help where help is needed?

Who do you think has suffered more during the current credit crunch – individuals or banks? Could banks do more to help families and small companies, as the UK government has urged them to do, or do you think that they would risk going out of business by being too generous?

Safeguards and rescue plans

Banks, like other financial organizations, operate best in what is called a free market. This term describes how the price of goods and services can rise or fall depending on availability, competition, new inventions and other factors. The opposite of a free market is government control, which means that political leaders decide how much things should cost, who should be able to buy them and so on.

Different approaches

A number of countries adopted communism during the twentieth century, which gave their governments full control of the economy. This style of government failed because it gave people no choice about what they could buy. Many things that people wanted were not available and the products which were for sale were often poorly made. China, which is still governed by communists, now allows private individuals to own companies; Russia abandoned communism altogether during the 1990s.

No country wants to adopt communism today, but as a result of the credit crunch, many people are calling for some government involvement in the banking industry. They argue that banks and other financial institutions need some help (including money) and guidance from governments. Some of these people believe that tough times call for tough solutions. Perhaps the only way to avoid another Great Depression is to strengthen defences against reckless banking practices.

Strengthening safeguards

Every industry, including banking, operates with some government restrictions. Most of the rules and restrictions are there to protect people from unfair practices or to help them retain confidence in banks generally. Some rules were brought in to avoid a repeat of the Great Depression (see pages 26-29); others developed when experts saw how dishonest people took advantage of new developments.

The aim of banking regulations is to maintain confidence in the industry as a whole. Depositors must believe that their money is safe, and if they have this confidence then banks can perform other services more successfully. Without enough deposits, banks cannot function and if lack of confidence leads to a run on banks, then the whole economy takes a downturn. The exact nature of the restrictions varies from country to country, but the most important rules ensure that a bank's business practices are reported accurately to the public.

The industry understands the need for regulation, which is why organizations such as the British Bankers' Association exist to monitor their own industry. Organizations outside the banking industry,

Whampoa Garden in Hong Kong is a shopping mall and collection of flats shaped like a huge ship. Since 1997, Hong Kong has been part of communist China, but the Chinese realize that profit-making developments such as Whampoa can bring wealth to the whole country.

such as the Treasury, Financial Services Authority and the Office of Fair Trading in the United Kingdom, act as watchdogs, setting out regulations and monitoring how banks play by the rules.

The problem is that in the wake of the fast-changing events of the credit crunch, rules need to be constantly amended, added and possibly dropped. Since so many of our financial industries are international, worldwide cooperation is needed. The Basel Committee on Banking Supervision was formed by central bank governors from ten powerful nations in 1974. It meets regularly to help governments (and central banks) develop plans and strategies to avoid – or minimize – banking crises in the future.

Rescue plans

Sometimes, especially during a credit crunch, governments feel that they need to rescue important areas of the economy for the good of the country. The Bank of England and the British government took such a step with the Northern Rock Bank, which was threatened with closure as a result of the US sub-prime mortgage crisis (see pages 30-33). In September 2007, the Bank of England used £10 billion to reduce the amount that Northern Rock owed on these toxic debts. Meanwhile, the government looked for someone to buy the bank and take over these debts. In February 2008, the British government bought the bank itself, in effect nationalizing it.

In the autumn of 2008, the United States agreed to a $700 billion (£466 billion) rescue, or bail-out, plan for the financial industry there. This vast sum of money would be pumped into banks and other institutions that had toxic debts arising from reckless lending earlier in the decade. This move had to be approved by the US Congress

YOUR MONEY'S WORTH

Big bad bail-outs?

Some people believe that big bail-outs such as that for Northern Rock in the UK and the $700 billion plan in the United States are unfair. They believe that taxpayers should not have to pay for mistakes made by greedy and reckless people in the banking industry.

Other people say that although these sums are hard to afford, the alternative – doing nothing and allowing bank after bank to go out of business – would be devastating. What do you think?

Personal account

NOT AGAIN!

Eighty-year-old Londoner June Dean withdrew the £10,000 she had saved with Northern Rock in autumn 2007. Feeling lucky that she had retained her savings, she then invested it with Bradford & Bingley (a bank that had been a building society until 2000). Then, in September 2008, her savings were threatened again when Bradford & Bingley ran into trouble. She decided to withdraw the £10,000 again, but she was less confident that she would find somewhere safe to invest it: 'I took my money out of Northern Rock and put it in here. Now I'm trying to decide which building society will be ruined next.'

(equivalent to the UK parliament) which withheld approval for some time because many felt that giving banks the money was rewarding them for their previous greed and recklessness. After the payout was approved, representatives of America's hard-hit car-making industry also appealed for financial help. Many Americans believe that ordinary people (who played no part in creating the crisis but who are suffering because of it) should really be given some of this money instead.

Barack Obama speaks in October 2008 during his US presidential campaign. Within a month of becoming president in January 2009 he had set in motion a $700 billion (£500 billion) plan to rescue the US from its economic problems.

Looking ahead

Banks still perform some of the same functions they have performed for thousands of years – offering funding and security for deposits – but they have changed rapidly in the past 20 years. Few people in the 1960s, for example, could have imagined using cash machines or transferring money online. Fewer still could imagine a world in which cash would hardly exist – and yet many experts predict such a future.

Cloudy crystal balls

Until about 2005, banking experts looking at the future would have examined the recent past and made some confident predictions. They would have noted that banking, like many industries, was growing and profitable. And, like other industries, it would be able to provide services based on newer – and cheaper – technologies.

The economic downturn since 2007 has caused the experts to revise their opinions. While it is true that banks are likely to broaden the nature of their services (with more online transactions, for example) they will probably have to pass on the costs of these developments to their customers. Many banking analysts foresee a future of high-tech but costly services.

In the newer, tougher economic climate people might be prepared to pay a bit extra for their banking services. But what they will want in return might be different from their needs in the past. Quick profits and cheap loans will probably mean less banking security. If people feel that their funds – and the bank in which they are held – are secure, then they will remain confident in the banking industry.

Some surprises

One of the most surprising banking developments is being led by some of the poorest nations in Africa. Communications and banking experts in Europe and North America constantly talk about how wireless technology will play a big role in the future. That future has already arrived in parts of Africa, especially in countries that never had a widespread traditional landline telephone system.

From 1999 to 2004, the number of mobile phone users in Africa jumped from 7.6 million to 82 million, with numbers growing by more than 60 per cent each year. Africans are using their phones to overcome the obstacles that prevented them from opening bank accounts, such as poor roads and political unrest. One fast-growing area is mobile banking, or using a mobile phone to transfer funds from one account to another or to pay for goods.

A Masai herdsman in rural Kenya stays in touch with his mobile phone. The economy in many parts of Africa now relies on mobile-phone technology – especially in areas which are a long way from banks and shops.

Glossary

bad debt Money that is owed (for example, to a bank) but which is impossible to collect because the borrower cannot repay it.

barter To exchange goods rather than paying for goods with money.

base rate The interest rate set by a central bank.

boom A time of economic growth.

building society A bank-like organization that is owned by its members.

Chancellor of the Exchequer The highest-ranking British government official in charge of finance and the economy.

commercial bank The most common type of bank, which takes people's savings and arranges loans.

communism A political system in which all property is owned by the community. A communist government provides work, health care, education and housing, but may deny people certain freedoms.

credit A banking term to describe lending and how easy it is to arrange it.

credit crunch A period, beginning in 2007, in which credit and other economic measures were severely affected.

currency The money that a country uses.

estate agent Someone who arranges the buying and selling of houses.

Fannie Mae (the Federal National Mortgage Association) Along with Freddie Mac, one of two large US government-supported mortgage organizations.

foreclose To take over property or shut down a business when a borrower can no longer meet loan repayments.

Freddie Mac *see* **Fannie Mae**

free market An economy in which businesses operate with little government control.

Great Depression The severe worldwide economic crisis from 1929 to 1939.

inflation A period of increasing prices, during which the value of money – ie what it can actually buy – goes down. Hyperinflation is an extreme form of inflation, when prices rise by more than 50 per cent every month.

interest rate The extra amount of money that borrowers pay back on a loan; also, the extra amount that a bank pays to a saver.

investment bank A bank that helps businesses raise money by investing in stocks.

loan An amount of money borrowed from a bank which must be repaid in full over an agreed period.

merge   To join together.

mortgage   A loan used to pay for a house.

nationalize   To transfer ownership to a national government.

offshore bank   A bank based in a country or region with few banking regulations.

overhead   Costs such as wages and rents that a company pays to operate.

private bank   A bank that looks after the affairs of very wealthy people.

profit   The overall amount of money a bank or other company receives minus the costs it pays out when supplying goods or services.

recession   A period of severe economic decline lasting six months or more.

run   A widespread move to withdraw money from a bank.

salary   Someone's regular pay.

stock   A percentage share in a company; stocks are like savings for many people but their value can fall rather than increase if the company is unsuccessful. A stock market is a meeting place where stocks are bought and sold.

sub-prime mortgage   A mortgage offered to someone who might not be able to repay it.

toxic debt   Money (from risky loans) that a bank might never receive.

Treasury   The branch of the British and other governments that looks after the national economy.

Further reading

Banking (How Economics Works) Barbara Allman (Lerner, 2005)

Banks Margaret C. Hall (Heinemann, 2007)

So You Want to Work In Banking and Finance? Margaret McAlpine (Hodder Wayland, 2005)

Websites

BBC glossary of credit crunch terms
http://news.bbc.co.uk/1/hi/business/
7618653.stm

The Tooth Fairy and the economy
http://money.uk.msn.com/investing/articles/article.
aspx?cp-documentid=9500362

What's so scary about the credit crunch?
http://news.bbc.co.uk/cbbcnews/hi/newsid_
7620000/newsid_7623300/7623384.stm

KidsBank
http://www.kidsbank.com/index_3.asp

Index